THE THUNDER, PERFECT MIND
Voice of the Divine Feminine

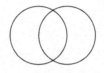

T0019580

© estate of Lee Lozowick, 2023

All rights reserved. No part of this book may be reproduced in any manner without written permission from the publisher, except in the case of quotes used in critical articles and reviews.

Cover Design: Hohm Press

Interior Design and Layout: Becky Fulker, Kubera Book Design, Prescott, Arizona

Library of Congress Control Number: 2023936556

ISBN: 978-1-942493-81-5

Hohm Press
P.O. Box 4410
Chino Valley, AZ 86323
800-381-2700
http://www.hohmpress.com

This book was printed in the U.S.A. on recycled, acid-free paper using soy ink.

THE THUNDER, PERFECT MIND
Voice of the Divine Feminine

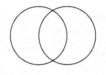

An Innocent Rendering by Lee Lozowick
Introduction by Mary Angelon Young

Contents

Introduction

Imagine for a moment that you look out on a limitless view—standing on a high mountain ledge, perhaps, or at the shore of an ocean—and you are bathed in silence. As your heart opens, your mind also expands into the vast space of sky. Resting there, a voice resounds around and within you. Suddenly your senses are alive, vibrant and thrilling. You shiver with recognition.

"Listen," she calls out, unmistakably feminine and unquestionably sovereign. "Take heed," she commands. "I am all beginnings and all endings! I am the harlot and the priestess. I am the one who is praised and who is ridiculed," she declares, "I am completely foolish and ultimately wise."

Instinctively, you know she is the Great One of many names—the Mother Goddess, Shakti, Isis, Sophia. Achingly human and fully divine, she trembles at her own fierce exultation. Her declarations are lament and jubilation, harmony and dissonance, sameness and contradiction, alien and familiar, beyond the binary of gender. She is all apparent opposites, and yet none of them defines or limits her. How can it be?

Her words roll forth as waves crashing against a bulwark. Inexplicably, as you listen, an inner door opens to a place of refuge beyond your comprehension. In her dance of opposites you are welcomed and disarmed, left groundless, and yet ground appears, firm beneath your feet. She is beyond time, and yet she is here, right now. At the still center of this thundering revelation, you are cradled in wonder, awestruck, devastated, even as you know yourself to be ultimately loved.

As a person of modernity, imagine such a direct encounter with *The Thunder, Perfect Mind*, recorded for posterity in Coptic around 200 CE and discovered, along with a cache of ancient texts, at Nag Hammadi in 1945. Forbidden by the Church and buried for almost two thousand years, like a time capsule awaiting the right moment, these secret treasures (including the Gospels of Mary Magdalene, Thomas, and Philip) rocked the world.

In 1978 a translation of *Thunder* by George MacRae became widely available, published in *The Nag Hammadi Library*.[1] Studied mostly by scholars, historians and theologians at the time, *Thunder's* inexplicable poetry shed light on the goddess traditions that were the fabric of daily life for thousands of years throughout the Middle East and Old Europe. Then, in 1981 Elaine Pagels published *The Gnostic Gospels*, revealing *The Thunder, Perfect Mind* to a broader readership and capturing the imagination of not only academicians but ordinary people called by a longing for something long lost in the religions and spirituality of the West.

When the American spiritual teacher Lee Lozowick (1943-2010) came across Pagel's work in the mid 1980s, he absorbed its poetry and transmission. A passionate student of mystical teachings both East and West, Lee was

---

[1]   *The Nag Hammadi Library*, James M. Robinson, editor, Harper-Collins, 1978.

inspired to offer his own rendering of *Thunder* in a version he described as "innocent."

This one word is a hint; it points toward the nondual essence of *Thunder*—the stainless, primordial nature of original being, which is everything and nothing, empty and full, existing in time and yet eternal, all at once. There, at the tangent point of spirit and matter, is a place of revelation where the quest of "who am I?" is radically intuited as something wondrous, spontaneous and free. It is the origin of existence, the secret heart of life—the place where we wear with natural ease the divine face, given long before we wore the iron masks and shackles of modernity.

The ancient world

The Thunder, Perfect Mind was brought to life in the ancient world at a time of seething change, when matrilineal civilizations were aggressively conquered, their mother goddesses replaced by the sky god cultures that gave rise to our world of today. Despite its suppression, *Thunder* was avidly studied by outlaw monks and renunciates of the Catholic Church until it was completely banned as heresy around 400 CE when someone—possibly the renegades of the Gnostic sects still active at the time—buried the text along with other forbidden scriptures.

The systematic repression of feminine divinity spread like a pandemic, shutting down temples and vast spiritual traditions until, over time, the goddess—worshipped by countless names like Astarte, Arduinna, Artemis, Cybele—went underground. Hidden in grottos, groves, and springs, in ruins and remnants of myth and story, glimmering faintly in remote places, she was kept barely alive in palliative images of Mary, mother of Jesus, in the shrines and cathedrals of Europe, or morphing from the beloved goddess Brigid of the Celts into Saint Brigit of Celtic Christianity.

Her presence remained, strangely available but arcane, in the great church of Hagia Sophia, the "Wisdom" of the Greek philosophers in Constantinople, now Istanbul in Turkey. She became even more ethereal and obscure in the Christian "Holy Ghost," the Hebrew Shekinah, or "presence of God," and in the mystical grail of Arthurian legend. During the centuries of the Inquisition, her worship in any form was reduced to a crime punished by torture and death by burning. Her presence receded further, alive in the beauty, constant change, and pristine powers of nature.

Today, *Thunder* remains mysterious. As a poem written in Coptic, *Thunder* is clearly connected with the great Isis tradition of Egypt. And yet, in the original translation she states, "I am the wisdom of the Greeks and the knowledge of the Barbarians…" and, because of this, some assume that she is the voice of Sophia, or the "Wisdom" of the Greeks. It's also thought that she emerged from the myths of Gnosticism as the voice of Barbēlō, the divine feminine and first spiritual entity to emerge from the Absolute.

Gnosticism is a collection of philosophy, religious beliefs, and mythology that coalesced near the end of the first century CE but has its roots in distant eras. The word gnostic comes from the Greek root, *gnōstikós*, meaning "having knowledge." *Thunder* rings true to Gnosticism's gender equality and worship of the divine feminine in a cosmology where Barbēlō gives birth to herself as a profusion, a flood, an overflow of the Supreme Reality.

Some scholars of Gnostic scripture and practitioners of Gnosis today say that the strange name, "Barbēlō," may have roots in the Coptic verb *berber*, "to overflow or boil over." It is now considered possible and even likely that Jesus, Mary Magdalene, John the Baptist and their disciples were essentially of the Gnostic persuasion. Certainly, they had at least studied arcane cosmologies or were well aware of Gnostic cults, like the Essenes, as well as the profusion of teachings and myths that thrived across the ancient world of their times.

Rather than limiting *Thunder* to one tradition, looking through the lens of history gives a broader view: her voice speaks to everyone because she came out of the melting and merging of the times, when Hebrew, Egyptian and Greek traditions blended freely in the swirling cauldron of humanity. She belonged to everyone. In an interview with "Frontline, from Jesus to Christ," Elaine Pagels commented further.

The Thunder, Perfect Mind is a marvelous, strange poem. It speaks in the voice of feminine divine power, but one that unites all opposites. One that is not only speaking in women, but also in all people. One that speaks not only in citizens, but aliens, it says, in the poor and in the rich. It's a poem which sees the radiance of the divine in all aspects of human life, from the sordidness of the slums of Cairo or Alexandria, as they would have been, to the people of great wealth, from men to women to slaves. In that poem, the divine appears in every, and the most unexpected, forms ...

"Thunder Perfect Mind" may have been written in Egypt. It's probably written by somebody who knows the traditions of Isis, knows the traditions of the Jews. It shows that this movement grew up in a world in which Jewish, Egyptian, Greek, Roman traditions are mingled and mixing and well-known to many sophisticated people. All you had to do was travel around a city, like Carnac, and you saw all these images, and these various religions and these various cultures mixing.[2]

Listen, take heed!

Thunder delivers a powerful warning—the red flag of consequence. It is dangerous to turn our backs on the goddess. In our troubled times of great uncertainty and upheaval, bereft of a sacred relationship to Mother Earth and a recognition of the feminine dimension of soul, our buried grief bubbles up as anxiety, random fears, night sweats, sleep disorders, depression, anger, despair, strange symptoms and profound alienation. As we grapple with ongoing war, the stress of climate change and the crumbling decay of culture, religion, and worldviews that once kept order and ruled the day, the loss of an empowered and embodied feminine spirituality has had a disastrous effect upon humanity and the planet.

---

[2] https:\\www.pbs.org. "Frontline: from Jesus to Christ," Interview with Elaine Pagels.

In modernity we are stretched beyond our limits, wandering in an artificial world of cell phones, social media, internet and a multitude of addictions that distract us from the niggling sense that something is profoundly wrong. With the denigration of the feminine we are alienated from our own bodies and feelings, from children, from the holy events of birth and death, aging and the sacred cycles of natural life. Academia and science have slowly realized the stark result: a planet under siege, unpredictable and often disastrous changes in weather patterns, the desecration of water, earth, trees, animals, the death of entire species. Greed, racism, violence, cruelty beyond our imagining, all of it a pervasive sickness of the soul.

But then, if you are reading this book, you are already well aware of the consequences we now face. You have already heard her call. You have heard her voice as the cries of the Earth, in the waters and winds, in the land itself; in the volcano, the hurricane and tornado; across canyons and prairies and mountains; in fire, flood and drought, in the lone coyote's howl and pairs of ravens soaring on the wing. You have heard her voice in the sufferings of humankind, in war, strife, conflict, the plight of children and the very old. You have felt her loving presence in moments of beauty, awe and wonder, in moments of song, music, dance, meditation, rapture, creative works.

Like me, you have glimpsed her at the liminal edges of your life, when you've stood at the crossroad, borne terrible loss and heartbreak, felt the full play of sorrow and joy, the bittersweet taste of grief, the surge of renewal. You have seen her handiwork in the spread of midnight stars, the changing seasons, the blue morning glory, the monarch, the hummingbird and mountain lion. You have felt her touch sitting vigil at the bedside of a dying loved one, in rare gasps of sheer ecstasy, when waves of love roll in and crash upon you, body and soul, when the mind is stilled and the feeling heart takes over.

Calling us to return, she awakens a primordial memory alive in the depths our souls. She glimmers with mystery, existing before and after creation, but she sings her song in the meeting point of eternity and existence in time. There, betwixt and between, as the ancient Celts would say, she can be glimpsed. She is the still peace of oneness and the wild, ecstatic dance of creation's diversity. "I came forth from the power …" she exclaims. In shouting out her truth, she propels us beyond religion and dogma and into the heart of life.

A universal message

Her proclamations resound in scriptures, ceremonies, rituals, poetry and religious myths from around the world. The repetitive use of "I am" in *Thunder* is heard in the great teachings of the Vedas and Upanishads—*Tat Tvam Asi,* "I am That" or "Thou art That," and as *"So'ham,"* the mantra of the breath, which reverberates within us. "I am" is heard in the Bible as a booming declaration of innate divine power that signals awakened consciousness.

Echoes of *Thunder* can also be found in Zen koans—playful, profound, and perplexing to the rational mind—as well as countless nondual teachings found in Vajrayana Buddhism. Elaine Pagels commented: "The use of polar opposites is an attempt to transcend the intellect through paradox. By identifying polar opposites, the mind is driven in circles until it surrenders."[3]

Several years ago, a friend gave me a book that came to be a treasured companion—*The Recognition of Our Own Heart*, a rendering of a one-thousand-year-old *sutra*, known and revered as the Recognition philosophy from the Shaiva Tantra tradition of Kashmir, translated by Joan Ruvinsky. Here, I found another ancient text shedding light upon the voice of *Thunder*, resounding also in Ruvinsky's decision to use the feminine pronoun in translating from the Sanskrit.

She births Herself as the many who interchangeably play
the roles of objects and subjects, reciprocally adapting,
each of the many, even in their individual forms,
embodying the One, the One who condenses into mind
and its objects.
She confines Herself by the limits
of space, time, perfection, knowledge and action.[4]

Almost a century ago, C.G. Jung explored alchemy and the pairs of opposites, shedding light on a "transcendent function"—a graceful, unexpected third that arises in between the polarities. Today, holding the tension of the opposites remains an essential transpersonal practice that integrates lived experience, resulting in an expansion of

---

[3]   *www.pbs.org.* "Frontline: from Jesus to Christ," Interview with Elaine Pagels.
[4]   Joan Ruvinsky, *The Recognition of Our Own Heart*, Quebec: Babaji's Kriya Yoga and Publications, 2019

awareness, a greater capacity to be present in the face of Mystery.

Thunder tells us that familiar, easy answers to the questions that plague our fragile human lives will not reconcile our suffering—we must look deeper to discover "perfect mind." She is not offering release in the oblivion of nondual transcendence or the escape routes of organized religions. Her mystery is far greater. She is liminal in every way, existing in the both/and space. She lures us in—can we be big enough to hold these two seemingly disparate things, all at once?

Can we bear the tension as we are stretched, heated, transported beyond fear, confusion, and the strain of paradox? For it we do, she will take us beyond the opposites of good and bad, right and wrong, and into her infinite realm where all things are radically intuited as wave, flux, and flow, miraculous, wondrous, full of grace.

Speak me, sing me alive, for I am

People of ancient times were not so different from us. They endured the ravaging terrors of disaster, rape, heartbreak, hunger, unimaginable loss, confusion, the world gone mad. They wrestled with all the great unanswerable questions and concerns of human life. Why was I born, only to die? What is the purpose of this existence? In their search to find meaning in suffering, they were aching for refuge, for what is real, abiding, imperishable.

Unlike people of modernity, the mythic imagination was alive and real within them. The ancients embodied their myths through sacred theatre, in the literal enactments of mystery rites like those at Eleusis. As often as once a year, men and women stepped into the character of Persephone and were taken by Hades into the underworld. In the agony of separation, Persephone's loving mother, the great goddess Demeter, raged and grieved until all of nature began to wither and die, and the gods intervened. Eventually, through her ordeal, Persephone became the queen of the underworld, who would spend six months a year above ground, when the natural world would flourish, bear fruit and seed. The other six months Persephone was confined with Hades in the hell-realm of the underworld, while leaves fell, trees grew barren, and icy winter lay solemn upon the earth. And so the seasons of nature were born, along with Persephone's knowledge of birth and death and rebirth, and the thread of life that linked them all.

In the mythic imagination of the ancient world, the gods spoke with thunder, the seal of their potency and force. The power of the word spoken aloud is undeniable across human culture. The word as logos, as creative force, gives form to our images of the divine—the *imago dei*—and leads us ultimately to the primordial, pure awareness of the "I am."

Most certainly, *The Thunder, Perfect Mind* existed in antiquity as an oral tradition that was spoken or sung, as were most if not all sacred texts in Hellenistic Greece, in India, in Celtic and indigenous traditions around the world. When *Thunder* is spoken aloud or sung the goddess is breathed into the world, where she pulses in cycles and waves of life carried on the breath. She does not invite us into a transcendent realm "up there," a nirvana where no-thing exists, but into the harmonic song of spirit and matter—the place where creation happens. *Thunder's* "I am" does not lure us into getting lost in the complex labyrinth of existence but holds out a thread to follow on the journey of eternal becoming.

In the Vedas, she appears as the primordial goddess Vac; she is sound and vibration, she is the hum, the mantra, the word and the wild sweet song of existence. Chanting, singing and speaking *Thunder* aloud, the ancestors who celebrated her in invocations (and there were many!) opened the floodgates to a direct, personal experience of her supreme force. Imagine what it would be like to enter—body, mind and soul—into the ecstatic ritual enactments of ancient Greece and Egypt, when her song reverberated in soaring stone temples ablaze with torchlight, redolent with incense, vibrating with the melody of lyre, the haunting sound of the *aulos*, the rhythms of sistrum and drum.

As you read *Thunder*, let your imagination "run wild," weaving past into present in a timeless pattern of sound and rhythm and breath that lifts you beyond your ordinary state and into a Great Mystery. You might listen to the Phrygian mode played upon the *aulos* or double flute (recordings are widely available) and imagine the sacred utterance of *Thunder*, a song woven upon the universal loom of sound. Dreaming back in time, remember her voice lifted in poetry around a fire in the desert, as you listen under brilliant stars that glitter in the black vault of night. We huddle there together with our drums, lyres and reed aulos, singing, keeping the beat, bodies moving in spontaneous dance around the flames or sitting rapt in our woolen shawls, falling into rapture, breathing deeply the chill air, warmed by the blaze, bathed in the smoke of cedar and bitter herbs.

In the solitude of contemplative moments, reading *Thunder* aloud can bring the poetry of your own mythic imagination to life. Doing so, you tap into the innate power of symbolic language, called twilight language or *sandhya bhasa* in the Sanskrit traditions. The twilight language of *Thunder* speaks to us personally. She is here and now with us, not the echo of some remote God living in a distant realm but a living truth existing beyond time and yet fully embracing our existence in time.

The inherent power of *The Thunder, Perfect Mind* lies dormant, waiting to be awakened into pure presence, to transport you beyond the known—though for most of us, our experience will be framed by reading. How can we go beyond our intellectual understanding to penetrate the depth and power of this sacred text, to make it our own? An intellectual understanding is a good beginning that connects head with heart. If we approach reading as a kind of deep listening, a contemplative plummet down and in, something more becomes possible. Suddenly there is magic afoot!

Of course, we did not learn this kind of study as young students, molded for better or worse by the linear, rational ordeals of tests, rote learning, and textbooks. But within each of us there is a blueprint for the kind of focused attention, the honed receptive awareness, the intelligent curiosity that cracks the code or encryption of poetry meant to be spoken, chanted, sung. Then, we may enter into and embody the presence of "I am."

Then, diving into *Thunder* becomes a quest for the divinity within each person. To discover her for yourself, experiment with putting the poetry into your own words. Captured by the mood of *Thunder's* freedom, many people have been inspired to go beyond the various translations of the original into English and countless other languages to interpret the poetry, intuitively filling in the numerous blanks where the original texts were damaged. One of the most beautiful versions I have found is in poet Jane Hirshfield's wonderful edition, *Women in Praise of the Sacred*. Another can be enjoyed in *Desert Wisdom* by Neil Douglas-Klotz, in which he links the divine feminine of *Thunder* to the ancient Hebrew figure of Hokhmah.

You don't have to be a poet, a scholar or a spiritual teacher to put *Thunder* into your own words. A useful template for this is found in *lectio divina* of the Christian tradition—study as a method of spiritual practice (see the Study Guide at the back of the book, page 55). Through asking ourselves a series of contemplative questions, we move along pathways that connect intellect, feeling, and gnosis or immediate knowing. This is one way we may link subjective personal experience with the objective utterance of the feminine divinity who exists, after all, both "within and without."

When have I tasted this experience? How would I say this? When and how have I been touched by an inexplicable divine presence? These are strong questions posed in an interior process that brings to awareness our own lived experience of non-rational states of being—moments of wonder, awe, insight, rapture, or stillness—in which we have intuited the truth that vibrates from the words of *Thunder*. It's an inroad that taps the magic and power of the word to transmit wisdom: "the Word made Flesh." Letting *Thunder* seep into the wholeness of who we are, we integrate the transmission and, in the process, we make this poetry our own, which brings us back to the current version of *The Thunder, Perfect Mind*.

Wise innocence

When his version was written, Lee had it handwritten in calligraphy style; only a few copies were made. These virtually disappeared in the archival materials of his ashram in Arizona and were remembered by only a handful of his long-time students. Four decades after it was penned, Lee's heartfelt response to *The Thunder, Perfect Mind* is posthumously offered in praise of the goddess.

Using the language that was common to his times and influenced by his own wide-ranging study, Lee's version of *Thunder* captures aspects of his own essential teachings. Most essentially, it provides a doorway into his realization that the journey to awakening always leads the soul through the feminine dimension of our human experience. Some years after the present text was written, he wrote:

> The process is feminine, and the keys to the lock which imprisons Reality or Truth is in a feminine approach—with very gentle, humorous, patient, accepting relationships to it. We must give ourselves time to relax into this enlightenment, rather than trying to force it to take us over. If we approach

the Work as Woman, we may just discover something quite unexpected and surprising but no less delightful.[5]

In the same way, the ancient Greeks went through Persephone, Christians go through Mary the mother of Jesus; Hindus and yogis enter into the symbolic figures of Radha, Sita, and Parvathy. Vajrayana Buddhists meditate upon and visualize Tara and Vajrayogini within their own bodies. Over a lifetime, Lee was a champion of the goddess as wise innocence—the essential, benevolent reality of Creation. Seeing reality through the lens of this state of being is what Lee called enlightened duality or *sahaj samadhi*—the natural, innate condition of awareness, which rests upon the nondual field of oneness.

Lee often spoke about the hardship of coming times on Earth, and his vision of the future fueled his urgent pleas for the inner work that ignites the alchemy of transformation. Many truth tellers and visionaries of our day speak of a necessary spiritual revolution on planet Earth. It's a revolution that can only happen as we recognize the nature of reality as it is, which begs for a restoration of divinity through feminine wisdom contexts for the Sacred and the spiritual process itself.

With every man and woman who steps forward to

---

[5] Lee Lozowick, *Eccentricities, Idiosyncrasies and Sacred Utterances of a Contemporary Western Baul*, Chino Valley, Ariz., Hohm Press, 1999, 80-81.

stand for wise innocence, to rediscover or adore the goddess in her many qualities and expressions, humanity is redeemed. The opening of every heart and mind feeds into the world soul, becomes a current that moves collective humanity toward change, affecting all levels from local to global to cosmic. It is an evolution of consciousness that is vitally necessary if our species is to survive. For this reason, as his student and biographer, I believe this small volume would have pleased Lee a great deal.

My own spiritual path has been inspired, all along the way, by a longing for the presence of the goddess—the divinity who appears in many forms and images. Today, many years after his death, I feel a deep, tender gratitude for Lee: Here is a man of realization and wisdom, a man of our times who spoke on her behalf and called me toward her. I hope that Lee's poetry will move you as it has me. It has many useful portals—as an inspiration, a guide to the original translations, as a prayer, a sacred song, or a ritual of praise. Her words help the mind relax the grip that shuts down the knowing in our gut; her poetry is marvelously nourishing, an ambrosia for the soul.

Taken to heart, she will awaken inside you. But, a word of caution may be useful: If we try to linger and get comfortable again, she will not let us. Her edginess will lead us to the brink, where our notions of right and wrong, good and evil are ruptured. Too wild to tame, she stirs our deepest longings for reality as it is. She is not a puzzle to be solved. She is a mystery that must be lived in the very real texture and challenge of each ordinary moment, in a flow of awareness from situation to situation.

Even as he was supportive of tradition and traditional practice, Lee once said, "If you have a road map of the path, you won't be on the path." The wisdom of this truth must be earned to have real substance, for it lives at the heart of Perfect Mind. She offers no panacea or method but calls us into feeling, holy instinct, radical knowing. Sensing her exquisite presence, we can bear the burning deluge of an intimate relationship with the Divine. In this crucible we cannot merely doze, follow a prescribed path, rest in contentment or denial, for she jars us awake and into the Unknown.

Moments of peace will come and go, but as long as we are alive we live in the paradox of an ongoing process. Waking up, we may wonder at times, how could I have forgotten? And in that moment, we already have. And so, we approach with whatever humility we can muster. In innocence, with hearts and minds open, ready to receive the knowledge, once again, that we are already and always blessed, gold-tinged with grace, forever awash in the mercy and beauty of Her.

Mary Angelon Young
March 1, 2023
Triveni, Arizona

Lee Lozowick's Innocent Rendering of:

THE THUNDER, PERFECT MIND

from The Nag Hammadi Library

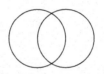

I was born out of the Lord
and I appear to those who seek me
and I am always in the midst of those who have found me
Look clearly at me, those of you to whom I have appeared
and hear me clearly, those who have ever heard me even
once
You to whom I belong, do not hesitate
and do not mask me from you
and do not make me poison in your speech or your mind
Do not cease to know me, ever
Pay attention!
Do not cease to know me.

I am all beginnings and all endings

I am the one who is praised and who is ridiculed

I am the harlot and the priestess

I am the woman of the world and the woman of the convent

I am the childbearer and the borne

I am the passion of woman

I am the ice of woman denied and many are her offspring

I am woman wed in splendor, yet I have no mate

I am the deliverer of the children, and she who has none

I am the ecstacy of my pain

I am both the bride and her mate, and it is he to whom
     I was born

I am she of whom my father was born and the sister of my
     mate[1]

and he is the one born of me

I am the slave of him to whom I bowed

I am the lord of the one born of me

But he is the one to whom I was born long before

And again he is born of me

And through him do I transcend

I am the center of his force when he is young

And he is the source of my life in my age

And what he feels is my demand

I am silence beyond all

and that which is remembered

I am speech heard by everyone

and sound in every realm

I am the very presence of my name[2]

Why do you who refuse my touch, crave it
    while you deny those who have it?
You who ignore me, beg me
And you who beg me, ignore me
You who speak of my wonder, live not of what you speak,
    and you who live apart from me express my wonder
You who have my heart, release it
    and those who have not my heart, offer it to them
For I am truth and illusion
I am ebbing and flowing.
I am free of all constraint, completely immoral, and I am
        all remorse
I am power and I am impotence
I am rage and I am calm

Pay attention and Remember[3]
I am beggar and I am king[4]

Pay attention to my filth and my oppulence
Do not reject me by your prejudice when I am no longer
    attractive,
  for you will see me again in other forms
And do not see me with vermin
  nor leave me isolated
And you will arrive at my doorstep
And do not see me when I am among the violent, nor the low
  do not misunderstand
And do not forsake me to the corpses of ignorance
But I, I am love and I am cruelty

Pay attention!
Do not despise my surrender
And do envy my discipline
When I am helpless do not forget me
When I am alive do not fear me
For why do you turn from me when I ail,
    and attack my waning strength
But I am she, the essence of weakness
    and the power of the downcast
I am she who fails and I live easily in success
I am completely foolish and ultimately wise.

Why have you failed to account for me in your lives?
For I shall rest in those who rest

And I shall arise in action

Why then have your eyes not seen and hearts denied?

    Because I am not of your pleasure?

I am the sight of your eyes, the beat of your heart and the

    delight of your pleasure

I am your opinion.

I am the idol of some,

And the smashed idol of the rest

I am the one who has always been shunned

And the one who has always been coveted

I am one they have called God

    and whom you call human

I am the one they have called truth

    and whom you call dream

I am the one whom you have sought
    And I am the one whom you have captured
I am the one whom you have banished
    and whom you have then called to return
I am the one to whom you have bowed
    and you have slaughtered reverence
I am she who knows no ritual
    And I am she who is ritual
I am the denial of the Divine
    And I am the one who knows the Lord
I am the one who has been revealed to you
and still you have turned away
I am the one you have already rejected
    and still you seek me

I am the one you have buried
   and you have not been able to leave me
   But whenever you are buried
   I will choose to stay with you
   And if you choose to stay with me
   I will not let you
Those who do not understand me, waste themselves.

Consume me from uselessness and sorrow
Consume me from that which lacks beauty
   and forget me in beauty
When in doubt, then consume me with strength, free of conflict
And whether in doubt or strength,
   Be what nothing can take root in.[4]

And be revealed to me, you to whom I have been revealed
    and you who know my lovers
And awaken conscience amongst those who are evolving
Evolve to the child
    and do not analyze its apparent weaknesses
And do not deny power because of form
For often the form is known from the power

And why do you deny me and then embrace me?
You have hurt and you have healed.
Do not change your mind from when you first knew me
And do not restrict others from knowing me
They turn you away and you know him not
And you know him and turn them away.

What is mine is known, when not known.
I know creation, and creation knows me.

But I am the thought of truth and all bodies
I am the answer to my question
    and the discovery of those who wander
    and the law of those who pray
    and the light of the sun of mine
        of those I have released
        and of gods at my command
        and of every creature's essence
        and of women who are my very soul
I am the one who is revered and blessed, and who is hated
    vehemently

I am the center

and the boundaries exist from me

And I am never here, and always here

I am the earth and I am the air

Those who are not blessed with my company have only death

    and those who have consumed me are the ones who live.

Those who are beside me have failed to acknowledge me

    And those who long for me know me well

When I am near you, you are distant

When I am distant, we are one

When I am outside of you, I am you.

When I am you, I am separate phenomena.

I am that out of which life arises,

I am death for those who die.

I am sense and senselessness.

I am creation, I am nothing.

I am the nurturing and I am barrenness

I am at the bottom

    and all are below me

I am Law and I am lawlessness

I am above all, pristine

    and sin is my child

I am passion in all rawness

And I am elegance in all circumstances

I am everyone's benefit

    and benediction which cannot be known

I am speechless in my speech

And profound in my silence

Know me in surrender, and feel me in struggle
I am she who aches with yearning
    and I am born amongst you
I cook food to feed the starving, inside
I understand my own name
I am the one who weeps
And the one wept to
I arise incomplete and complete in myself
And in completeness cannot stop disintegration
I am the one who is Whole
    and the one to whom sin is truth.
You respect me, and you plot against me
And you will triumph over those who overthrow me
Conquer them before you are the conquered

because the war is your subjectivity
If I condemn you, no hope
And if I give hope, you are free
For there are no distinctions
    and you are only what you are
And what is inside is outside, and he is both
And both are you
Pay attention
    and remember, you who attend to me
I am that attention.
I am that remembrance.
I am what everything is called
    and what the called is.
I am the vision of everything, and the nothing of the vision.

And I will endlessly be all and always be ending.
And light is my gift
Pay attention and remember.
I will unleash the unthinkable to you.
And this will not change me.

And I will still not be he who I was born of.
And I will show him to you.
And you will hear his voice.
And you will see his signs.
Pay attention you who read this
    and you also who hear of it
    and you who have ever heard of it.
For I am only Just This,[6]

and there is no one to understand
For there is a multitude of distractions in
    the pleasures of the senses
    and in the realms of being
    and failure to be true to the law
    and in the passing of phenomena
    which men seek endlessly until they die unsatisfied
And There I am, if they will bow at my feet now
    and they will Live, undying.

Endnotes

All cited page numbers refer to Lee Lozowick, *Hohm Sahaj Mandir Study Manual*, Volume I, Hohm Press, 1996.

1. **Gender.** Lee continues to elucidate the paradoxes and gender-bending revelations of the original text, taking the reader beyond the "normative" binaries and gender roles of our culture.

2. **Name.** Lee is referring to the power of all names of the Divine. In many religious traditions, such as the logos in Christianity and *nama* in Hinduism, as well as the practice of mantra (the repetition of sacred words or phrases), every name of the Divine has innate power that vibrates as the Divine in actuality. Lee's personal practice was the repetition of the name of his guru, the revered south Indian beggar saint, Yogi Ramsuratkumar, who gave his name as both blessing and mantra.

3. **Pay Attention and Remember.** One of Lee Lozowick's essential teaching phrases, pay attention and remember refers to a state of being that is the ground for all other practices on the spiritual path. Paying attention in this context tacitly implies that one's attention is upon Reality as what is, as it is, here and now. When paying attention and remembering, one's awareness and attention are free to be fully present in the moment, from "ground to sky."

    Paying attention and remembering is the natural, transpersonal link of the individual to the unified field of Life. To pay attention and remember is a functional practice of awareness spanning the seeming chasm between multiplicity and oneness, immanence and transcendence, matter and spirit.

    Remembrance is a powerful state of being; it is not something one does but something one is. It is a doorway to radical insight, wonder and revelation. To remember oneself is a tacit and spontaneous recognition of original being and the benevolence of the Divine. To "re-member" is to regain wholeness and integrity as a being in relationship with the One. [347]

    > This field of awareness includes not only that which you know consciously, but also that which you know psychically or unconsciously, which is pretty much everything. It includes one's whole genetic inheritance and so on. It's like being omniscient

but not knowing you're omniscient. The field of consciousness covers everything, every person—everything and anything that's going on in the world.... When you surrender attention into that field the Divine brings to consciousness that in your particular unique function and/or environment which is most optimal for you to be aware of in the moment. [334-338]

4. **Beggar and king.** The use of the terms "beggar" and "king" here are a reference to Lee's guru, the beggar saint, Yogi Ramsuratkumar.

5. **Be what nothing can take root in.** This phrase refers to the inner yoga or inner work that cultivates a state of remaining free in the midst of distraction, fascination and seduction. This is a formless practice that enables one to have free attention placed in a way that is most beneficial to oneself and to all of life—which is to follow and embody one's own dharma.

   …to be that in which nothing can take root, experientially and literally, is not just to be slippery or too fast moving for anything to "root" in you. You can be slippery like a stone at the bottom of a running stream, but algae grows on it, and then it's a hold for more algae. The point is that you be what nothing can take root in. Nothing. Not holiness, not negativism, nothing. You are that context itself. It's not even that you become that or learn that. You [already] are that—that in which nothing can take hold, in which no seeds can germinate. [162]

6. **Just This.** "Just This" is Lee's seminal expression of Assertion, in which the individual affirms a radical intuition of the truth of Ultimate Reality and the certainty that there is only God. (For more information on Assertion, see *Enlightened Duality* by Lee Lozowick and M. Young, noted in References.)

The Thunder, Perfect Mind
Translated by George W. MacRae

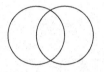

I was sent forth from the power,
and I have come to those who reflect upon me,
and I have been found among those who seek after me.
Look upon me, you who reflect upon me,
and you hearers, hear me.
You who are waiting for me, take me to yourselves.
And do not banish me from your sight.
And do not make your voice hate me, nor your hearing.
Do not be ignorant of me anywhere or any time. Be on
　　your guard!
Do not be ignorant of me.
For I am the first and the last.
I am the honored one and the scorned one.
I am the whore and the holy one.
I am the wife and the virgin.
I am <the mother> and the daughter.
I am the members of my mother.
I am the barren one
and many are her sons.
I am she whose wedding is great,
and I have not taken a husband.
I am the midwife and she who does not bear.
I am the solace of my labor pains.
I am the bride and the bridegroom,
and it is my husband who begot me.
I am the mother of my father
and the sister of my husband
and he is my offspring.
I am the slave of him who prepared me.
I am the ruler of my offspring.

But he is the one who begot me before the time on a
    birthday.
And he is my offspring in (due) time,
and my power is from him.
I am the staff of his power in his youth,
and he is the rod of my old age.
And whatever he wills happens to me.
I am the silence that is incomprehensible
and the idea whose remembrance is frequent.
I am the voice whose sound is manifold
and the word whose appearance is multiple.
I am the utterance of my name.

Why, you who hate me, do you love me,
and hate those who love me?
You who deny me, confess me,
and you who confess me, deny me.
You who tell the truth about me, lie about me,
and you who have lied about me, tell the truth about me.
You who know me, be ignorant of me,
and those who have not known me, let them know me.
For I am knowledge and ignorance.
I am shame and boldness.
I am shameless; I am ashamed.
I am strength and I am fear.
I am war and peace.
Give heed to me.
I am the one who is disgraced and the great one.
Give heed to my poverty and my wealth.

Do not be arrogant to me when I am cast out upon the
    earth,
and you will find me in those that are to come.
And do not look upon me on the dung-heap
nor go and leave me cast out,
and you will find me in the kingdoms.
And do not look upon me when I am cast out among those
    who
are disgraced and in the least places,
nor laugh at me.
And do not cast me out among those who are slain in
    violence.
But I, I am compassionate and I am cruel.
Be on your guard!
Do not hate my obedience
and do not love my self-control.
In my weakness, do not forsake me,
and do not be afraid of my power.
For why do you despise my fear
and curse my pride?
But I am she who exists in all fears
and strength in trembling.
I am she who is weak,
and I am well in a pleasant place.
I am senseless and I am wise.
Why have you hated me in your counsels?
For I shall be silent among those who are silent,
and I shall appear and speak,
Why then have you hated me, you Greeks?

Because I am a barbarian among the barbarians?
For I am the wisdom of the Greeks
and the knowledge of the barbarians.
I am the judgement of the Greeks and of the barbarians.
I am the one whose image is great in Egypt
and the one who has no image among the barbarians.
I am the one who has been hated everywhere
and who has been loved everywhere.
I am the one whom they call Life,
and you have called Death.
I am the one whom they call Law,
and you have called Lawlessness.
I am the one whom you have pursued,
and I am the one whom you have seized.
I am the one whom you have scattered,
and you have gathered me together.
I am the one before whom you have been ashamed,
and you have been shameless to me.
I am she who does not keep festival,
and I am she whose festivals are many.
I, I am godless,
and I am the one whose God is great.
I am the one whom you have reflected upon,
and you have scorned me.
I am unlearned,
and they learn from me.
I am the one that you have despised,
and you reflect upon me.
I am the one whom you have hidden from,
and you appear to me.

But whenever you hide yourselves,
I myself will appear.
For whenever you appear,
I myself will hide from you.
Those who have [...] to it [...] senselessly [...].
Take me [... understanding] from grief.
and take me to yourselves from understanding and grief.
And take me to yourselves from places that are ugly and
    in ruin,
and rob from those which are good even though in ugliness.
Out of shame, take me to yourselves shamelessly;
and out of shamelessness and shame,
upbraid my members in yourselves.
And come forward to me, you who know me
and you who know my members,
and establish the great ones among the small first creatures.
Come forward to childhood,
and do not despise it because it is small and it is little.
And do not turn away greatnesses in some parts from the
    smallnesses,
for the smallnesses are known from the greatnesses.
Why do you curse me and honor me?
You have wounded and you have had mercy.
Do not separate me from the first ones whom you have
    known.
And do not cast anyone out nor turn anyone away
[...] turn you away and [... know] him not.
[...].
What is mine [...].
I know the first ones and those after them know me.

But I am the mind of [...] and the rest of [...].
I am the knowledge of my inquiry,
and the finding of those who seek after me,
and the command of those who ask of me,
and the power of the powers in my knowledge
of the angels, who have been sent at my word,
and of gods in their seasons by my counsel,
and of spirits of every man who exists with me,
and of women who dwell within me.
I am the one who is honored, and who is praised,
and who is despised scornfully.
I am peace,
and war has come because of me.
And I am an alien and a citizen.
I am the substance and the one who has no substance.
Those who are without association with me are ignorant
    of me,
and those who are in my substance are the ones who know
    me.
Those who are close to me have been ignorant of me,
and those who are far away from me are the ones who have
    known me.
On the day when I am close to you, you are far away from
    me,
and on the day when I am far away from you, I am close
    to you.
[I am ...] within.
[I am ...] of the natures.
I am [...] of the creation of the spirits.

[...] request of the souls.
I am control and the uncontrollable.
I am the union and the dissolution.
I am the abiding and I am the dissolution.
I am the one below,
and they come up to me.
I am the judgment and the acquittal.
I, I am sinless,
and the root of sin derives from me.
I am lust in (outward) appearance,
and interior self-control exists within me.
I am the hearing which is attainable to everyone
and the speech which cannot be grasped.
I am a mute who does not speak,
and great is my multitude of words.
Hear me in gentleness, and learn of me in roughness.
I am she who cries out,
and I am cast forth upon the face of the earth.
I prepare the bread and my mind within.
I am the knowledge of my name.
I am the one who cries out,
and I listen.
I appear and [...] walk in [...] seal of my [...].
I am [...] the defense [...].
I am the one who is called Truth
and iniquity [...].
You honor me [...] and you whisper against me.
You who are vanquished, judge them (who vanquish you)
before they give judgment against you,

because the judge and partiality exist in you.
If you are condemned by this one, who will acquit you?
Or, if you are acquitted by him, who will be able to detain
    you?
For what is inside of you is what is outside of you,
and the one who fashions you on the outside
is the one who shaped the inside of you.
And what you see outside of you, you see inside of you;
it is visible and it is your garment.
Hear me, you hearers
and learn of my words, you who know me.
I am the hearing that is attainable to everything;
I am the speech that cannot be grasped.
I am the name of the sound
and the sound of the name.
I am the sign of the letter
and the designation of the division.
And I [...].
(3 lines missing)
[...] light [...].
[...] hearers [...] to you
[...] the great power.
And [...] will not move the name.
[...] to the one who created me.
And I will speak his name.
Look then at his words
and all the writings which have been completed.
Give heed then, you hearers
and you also, the angels and those who have been sent,
and you spirits who have arisen from the dead.

For I am the one who alone exists,
and I have no one who will judge me.
For many are the pleasant forms which exist in numerous
    sins,
and incontinencies,
and disgraceful passions,
and fleeting pleasures,
which (men) embrace until they become sober
and go up to their resting place.
And they will find me there,
and they will live,
and they will not die again.

From *The Nag Hammadi Library,* James M. Robinson, General Editor. Copyright © 1978, 1988 by E. J. Brill, Leiden, The Netherlands. Used by permission of HarperCollins Publishers.

Suggested Reading

The Chalice and the Blade, Riane Eisler, HarperCollins, 1987.

Desert Wisdom, Neil Douglas-Klotz, CreateSpace Independent, 2011.

Enlightened Duality, Lee Lozowick and M. Young, Hohm Press, 2008.

The Gnostic Gospels, Elaine Pagels, Random House, 1981.

The Gospel of Mary Magdalene, Jean-Yves Leloup, Inner Traditions, 2002.

The Great Goddess: Reverence of the Divine Feminine from the Paleolithic to the Present, Jean Markale, Inner Traditions, 1999.

The Nag Hammadi Library, James M. Robinson, editor, Harper Collins, 1990.

The Recognition of Our Own Heart, Joan Ruvinsky, Quebec: Babaji's Kriya Yoga and Publications, 2019.

When God Was a Woman, Merlin Stone, Mariner Books, 1978.

Women in Praise of the Sacred, Jane Hirshfield, editor, Harper Perennial, 1995.

Study Guide

The Thunder, Perfect Mind offers a doorway through which we can explore and expand our understanding and direct experience of the divine feminine through contemplation. One way to begin is through a process of asking questions that take us beyond the intellect and into a felt reality of the divine feminine as the universal force and foundation of life that permeates everything—beings, objects, patterns, processes and experiences. The poetry of *Thunder* prompts us to engage the challenge of paradox with curiosity and wonder. For example, *Thunder* invites us to open naturally into the understanding that the feminine is not limited to females or those who identify as females, or based on any identification on the spectrum of gender.

Here are a few examples of questions you might ask yourself, listening deeply for a response from within. Delve into them through writing, where your own voice can be revealed. You may wish to engage these questions with others, or simply reflect on them in silence.

What feelings, intuitions, questions or reactions arise for me reading *The Thunder, Perfect Mind*?

What are my core beliefs about the feminine nature of the Divine?

How do I experience feminine ways of being and spiritual growth?

How is the divine feminine expressing through my life in the present time? In the past?

The paradoxes in this text are many. What does meeting paradox evoke in me? How comfortable am I with paradox of a spiritual nature?

What are the pairs of opposites at play in my life at this time? What pairs of opposites have been active in my past?

What is the middle ground between any two of the opposing possibilities, decisions or concepts in my life?

Try standing in the middle, open and relaxed and curious, in the "in between." Let go of identifying with either side of a paradoxical polarity. Let go of any position or concept of being right. How does this experience feel? What insight or intuition arises?

About Lee Lozowick

Born in New Jersey in 1943, after a sudden awakening Lee Lozowick burst onto the American spiritual scene in 1975 offering an authentic, fresh alternative to the New Age spirituality of the times. To the hippies of the day he proposed what seemed like the opposite of freedom in his teaching of "spiritual slavery," in which one aspired to live a radical surrender to the Will of God here and now as "Just This"— the nondual affirmation of recognizing and accepting what is present in this moment, as it is.

Lee was a visionary who founded three ashrams (in Arizona, France and India) and established the Baul Path in the West, introducing his students and many other Westerners to the traditions and practice of the Bauls of Bengal, India—a revolutionary tantric sect of wandering beggars, singers, dancers and lovers of God. In this 500-year-old path Lee recognized the purest reflection of his own revelations on the path, as well as a means to communicate ages-old, Eastern teachings in a way that was moving, current to our times, and deeply grounded. Lee was a teacher, guru, friend, poet and lyricist, as well as a beloved father, a rock & roll singer and a lover of sacred art. First and foremost, he considered himself the long-time devotee and "heart son" of Yogi Ramsuratkumar (1918-2001), the revered beggar-saint of Tiruvannamalai, south India, with whom he enjoyed a deep spiritual love and profound intimacy of the spirit.

How spiritual slavery and a radical reliance on the Divine could be lived in the practical world of function and form was evident in Lee's life and work. While guiding the sadhana of his students, managing businesses, keeping a grueling schedule of travel and teaching, and attending to the personal needs of his large extended family, Lee deepened and intensified a fiery love for the Divine, directed through the tangent point of his master, Yogi Ramsuratkumar. Lee was a living embodiment of what he taught: his presence transmitted the profound relaxation of being that arises from radical faith and trust in Divine Intelligence and the infinite power and sheer magic of Grace as the mover of all the details of life—the places and things that absorb our human attention, even down to basic needs for food, clothing, and shelter.

His teachings are preserved in several dozen books, hundreds of talks and seminars given in the U.S., Mexico, India and throughout Europe. Lee's most poignant teachings can be found in three large volumes of devotional poetry written to Yogi Ramsuratkumar and encoded in the poetry of scores of song lyrics written for his several rock and blues bands. His abiding love and reverence for beauty and art was expressed in his personal collections of sacred art and in the beauty and divine mood of his ashrams. At the root of it all, Lee Lozowick inspired many with his nondual assertion, "There is only God," which is the foundation for his tantric teachings on Enlightened Duality, his lifelong devotion to Divinity and the truth of a personal Beloved existing beyond forms and genders.

As long as four decades ago, Lee saw the urgent need for a return of sacred culture, simplicity, and the wise use of resources, which depends upon individual awakening of awareness to our innate human condition of "organic innocence." As the crucible and ground of transformation on the spiritual path, ordinary daily life becomes uplifted in conscious relationship (*The Alchemy of Love and Sex* remains one of his most widely read books) and conscious parenting (his book by the same name is acknowledged as a classic).

A warrior of spiritual discipline himself, Lee supported no easy, "quick-fix" solutions to the pain of human suffering. Rather, he guided his students toward building a firm foundation in life through personal integrity and traditional practice—meditation, contemplative and devotional practices such as mantra and chanting, creativity, and a ruthless self-honesty in working with mind and emotions. Along with simplicity of healthy diet and exercise, he advocated for right livelihood and sexuality as the only sane alternative to a life of comfort-driven, blind selfishness. He begged his students and friends to turn unceasingly to the Source of All, within one's own heart and through the divine agency of the One.

A distinguishing element of the Baul tradition is an open-minded, universal perspective that draws wisdom from a "patchwork" of authentic paths and traditions. As Western-style Baul, Lee was committed to conversation and connection between spiritual and religious traditions, and in this regard he often traveled with his students to seek out wise dignitaries of our age. In the 1990s, he encouraged the organization of a conference titled "Crazy Wisdom and Divine Madness" in Boulder, Colorado—a gathering of Tibetan Buddhist rinpoches, lamas, and teachers, Christian contemplatives, and Hindu tantrikas. In his early sojourns to India (1977-1986), Lee sought out and met many obscure yogis and individuals of sublime realization as well as the great ones of the times: Anandamayi Ma, Baba Muktananda, Tat Walla Baba, Sai Baba, J. Krishnamurti and, of course, his own master, Yogi Ramsuratkumar. Years later, he would establish friendships and collaboration with Baul masters Sanatan Das Thakur Baul and Purna Das Baul. Traveling extensively in the West, Lee developed friendships with a wide range of contemporary teachers. His eclectic activities with his own students was kaleidoscopic, spanning from the cafés and cathedrals of Europe to the sweat lodges of indigenous elder Grandfather Raymond in California, to visiting Zen monasteries or attending public talks, where they met— and often befriended—teachers like Richard Baker Roshi, Maesumi Roshi, and Jakusho Kwong Roshi to mention only a few. On annual visits to California, Lee often took students to meet with Sufi teacher Llewellyn Vaughan-Lee in Point Reyes and radical visionary E. J. Gold near Sacramento. In France, Lee introduced his students to his longtime close friend and collaborator, the renowned spiritual teacher/filmmaker, Arnaud Desjardins, a disciple of Swami Prajnanpad, as well as Yvan and Nadege Amar and their guru, Chandra Swami.

In the summer of 1975 Lee founded Hohm Press as a means of sharing his teaching with spiritual seekers of the time. Since then, the press has continued to publish Lee's books while expanding to encompass works in many different fields, including religious studies, parenting, yoga, transpersonal psychology, and children's books on health and nutrition (through its affiliate Kalindi Press). Foreign-language editions of Lee's books have also been published in German, French, Portuguese, Spanish, Hungarian and Romanian.

An uncompromising stand for the unified oneness of life, "kindness, generosity and compassion" in relationship, a call to "pay attention and remember," to know the ecstatic truth of our essential nature and discover that "the only Grace is loving God" were hallmarks of Lee Lozowick's life and his teaching. These remain at the center of his immense legacy to his students, followers of all spiritual and transformational paths, his readers, colleagues and friends. Lee died on November 16, 2010. His body is interred in the samadhi temple at Triveni Ashram in Arizona. His ashrams continue today, maintained by his students. For more information visit hohmsahajmandir.org online.

About Mary Angelon Young

Mary Angelon Young, M.S. is a writer, workshop leader, and longtime traveler on the spiritual path. Her eleven books on spirituality, biography and the Indian traditions—as well as more recent forays into historical fiction with a spiritual bent—are enriched by decades of pilgrimage in India and Europe and a lifelong passion for the mythic and wisdom traditions of the world. As a close disciple of Lee Lozowick for many years, she traveled extensively with him and served as his appointed biographer. Mary Angelon lives at Triveni Ashram in the high desert of Arizona with her husband Thomas. For more information about workshops and books, visit her website and blog at www. maryangelonyoung.com

About Hohm Press

HOHM PRESS is committed to publishing books that provide readers with alternatives to the materialistic values of the current culture, and promote self-awareness, the recognition of interdependence, and compassion. Our subject areas include parenting, transpersonal psychology, religious studies, women's studies, the arts and poetry.

Contact Information: Hohm Press, PO Box 4410, Chino Valley, Arizona, 86323, USA; 800-381-2700, or 928-636-3331; email: publisher@hohmpress.com

Visit our website at *www.hohmpress.com*